WHAT WILL YOU MAKE ROOM FOR IN YOUR WAGON?

and

TAKING UPON US HIS NAME

WHAT WILL YOU MAKE ROOM FOR IN YOUR WAGON?

and

TAKING UPON US HIS NAME

Ardeth G. Kapp

CLASSIC TALK SERIES

Deseret Book Company
Salt Lake City, Utah

Reprinted with permission.

Library of Congress Catalog Card Number: 98-72596
ISBN 0-87579-976-0

Printed in the United States of America

10 9 8 7 6 5 4 3 2 1 72082 - 6015

WHAT WILL YOU MAKE ROOM FOR IN YOUR WAGON?

I am grateful, brothers and sisters, for the privilege of being on this campus and participating in any way in the mission of this university and your part in it as you accept the opportunity to learn and prepare to go forth and serve. The thoughts I would like to share with you today I believe fit under the title "What Will You Make Room for in Your Wagon?" It might be considered a self-talk message for my benefit as well as for yours.

A number of years ago, when I was a beginning teacher in elementary school, I had the superintendent's daughter in my fourth-grade class. She had some learning difficulties. I was anxious for her to learn as quickly as possible. After many attempts with only a blank stare in response to my efforts to teach her long division, at one moment she jumped up and excitedly announced, "Finally you said it right. I've got it. I've got it." I pray that the Spirit of the Lord will bless us so that the things I have prepared will be of help to you.

DRAWING FROM OUR TIME BANK

Some time ago, one of the students on this campus called my home to report what sounded to me like a condition of epidemic proportions. It was just before finals. Shelly, who happens to be my niece, explained that she and her roommates were stressed out and needed a place to escape for the weekend. I, of course, was delighted to provide the place. They said there had hardly been a weekend or even a day when they had not been completely overloaded. "So much to do and so little time" was their comment as they talked of schedules, commitments, expectations, pressures, and even some anxieties about dates, deadlines, decisions, finances, future obligations, and unlimited opportunities.

With so many wonderful opportunities, maybe you could take advantage of it all if you could stay up long enough, get up early enough, run fast enough, and live long enough. It has been said that if you're willing to burn the candle at both ends, you might get by, but only if the candle is long enough.

We all seem to be looking for ways to do more faster. Nowadays we can watch one TV show while we tape another and fast forward to eliminate the commercials. We read condensed books and eat fast foods. Some would have us believe that the more appointments we have in our day planner, the more successful we are. The plague of our day is the thought repeating in our minds like the steady ticking of a clock: "I do not have time. I do not have time." And yet we have all there is.

Today we read of stress management, the Epstein-Barr syndrome, overload, and over-exhaustion. In an effort to escape some of the pressures of our day, we see an increased consumption of alcohol, the improper use of prescription drugs, other related social ills, immorality, and even suicide. And yet never before has there been such evidence of increased knowledge and expanding opportunities. It has been said that "we have exploded into a free-wheeling, multiple-option society" (John Naisbitt, *Megatrends* [New York: Warner Books, 1982], introduction, xxiii). We are faced with the burden of too many choices. I have discovered that even the purchase of a simple tube of toothpaste poses many options considering brand, flavor, size, cost, ingredients, and promises. We speak of high tech and high touch, hardware and software, and find we need increasing self-reliance as the options multiply at an accelerated pace.

William James, the noted American psychologist and philosopher, states:

> Neither the nature nor the amount of our work is accountable for the frequency and severity of our breakdowns, but their cause lies rather in those absurd feelings of hurry and having no time, in that breathlessness and tension; that anxiety . . . , that lack of inner harmony and ease. [Quoted by William Osler in *A Way of Life* (New York: P. B. Hoeber, 1937), 30.]

Too often we allow ourselves to be driven from one deadline, activity, or opportunity to the next. We check events off our calendar and think, "After this week things will let up" or "After this semester" or "After graduation, then the pressure will ease." We live with false expectations. Unless we learn to take control of the present, we will always live in anticipation of better days in the future. And when those days arrive, we shall still be looking ahead, making it difficult to enjoy the here and now. The beautiful fall leaves come and go, and in our busyness we miss them. "Given another season, we'll do better," we say.

We live in a time when we can do more, have more, see more, accumulate more, and want more than in any time ever known. The adversary would keep us busily engaged in a multitude of trivial things in an effort to keep us distracted from the few vital things that make all of the difference.

When we take control of our lives, we refuse to give up what we want most, even if it means giving up some of what we want now. Former BYU president Jeffrey R. Holland reminded students to "postpone your gratification so you don't have to postpone your graduation" (Jeffrey R. Holland, "The Inconvenient Messiah," in *BYU Speeches, 1981–82,* 82). And how is this to be accomplished?

I believe the most destructive threat of our day is not nuclear war, not famine, not economic disaster, but rather the despair, the discouragement, the despondency, the defeat caused by the discrepancy between what we believe to be right and how we live our lives. Much of the emotional and social illness of our day is caused when people think one way and act another. The turmoil inside is destructive to the Spirit and to the emotional well-being of one who tries to live without clearly defined principles, values, standards, and goals.

Principles are mingled with a sense of values. They magnify each other. Striving to live the good life is dependent upon values to measure our progress as we learn to like and dislike what we ought to. We learn to be honest by habit, as a matter of course. The question shouldn't be "What will people think?" but "What will I think of myself?" We must have our own clearly defined values burning brightly within. Values provide an inner court to which we can appeal for judgment of our performance and our choices.

We live in a time when too often success is determined by the things we gather, accumulate, collect, measure, and even compare in relation to what others gather, accumulate, collect, measure, and compare. This pattern of living invites its own consequences and built-in stress. Maybe you heard of the woman who received a call from her banker explaining that she was overdrawn, to which she promptly replied, "No, sir, I am not overdrawn. My husband may have underdeposited, but I am not overdrawn."

It is possible that we try to overdraw from our time bank and suffer the nagging and debilitating stress of bankruptcy. The difference, however, is more significant than our money bank. Only twenty-four hours a day is deposited for an indefinite period of time. No more and no less.

It is as we learn to simplify and reduce, prioritize, and cut back on the excesses that we have enough time and money for the essentials, for all that we ultimately want in the end.

THE VALUE OF CAREFUL PRUNING

This fall some friends came to our home with their children and brought with them a case of the most beautiful, large peaches I have ever seen. They were almost unbelievable in their size, their beauty, and their flavor. Brother Pitt explained that they had just won first prize at the county fair for their peaches, and they had an orchard full of them. I asked how you produce such remarkable fruit, and the family was eager to explain. "We learned how to prune the peach trees and thin the weak fruit," they said. "It's hard work and must be done regularly."

"We also learned what happens when you don't prune," said one of the children. Their father had wisely suggested that three trees in the orchard be left to grow without the harsh results of the pruning knife. They explained to me that the fruit from these trees was not only very small in size but did not have the sweet taste of the other fruit. The lesson was obvious. There was no question in their minds about the far-reaching value of careful pruning.

McKinley Tabor recently spoke at an ethics conference at the BYU Marriott School of Management. In an article entitled "Misplaced Pride," based on his talk, he reflected regretfully on some misplaced priorities. Mr. Tabor said:

> I was aggressive in wanting to own things, in wanting to make a lot of money, in wanting to be the big duck in a little pond. Now I focus on things like my children, on my family life in general, on experiencing things instead of owning things. I like to go places and see new things and meet new people where before I liked to own cars and have big bank accounts. The things that are important to me now are things that stay with you a lot longer than a dollar bill. [McKinley Tabor, "Misplaced Pride," *BYU Today*, July 1989, 17–19.]

In the book *The Star Thrower,* Loren Eiseley writes of the beaches of Costabel and tells how the tourists and professional shell collectors, with a kind of greedy madness, begin early in the morning in their attempts to outrun their less-aggressive neighbors as they gather, collect, and compete. After a storm, people are seen hurrying along with bundles, gathering starfish in their sacks. Following one such episode, the writer says:

> I met the star thrower. . . .
>
> . . . He was gazing fixedly at something in the sand.
>
> Eventually he stooped and flung the object beyond the breaking surf. . . .
>
> . . . "Do you collect?" [I asked.]
>
> "Only like this," he said softly. . . ."And only for the living." He stooped again, oblivious of my curiosity, and skipped another star neatly across the water.
>
> "The stars," he said, "throw well. One can help them." . . .
>
> . . . For a moment, in the changing light, the sower appeared magnified, as though casting larger stars upon some greater sea. He had, at any rate, the posture of a god. . . .
>
> I picked [up] and flung [a] star. . . .
>
> . . . I could have thrown in a frenzy of joy, but I set my shoulders and cast, as the thrower in the rainbow cast, slowly, deliberately, and well. The task was not to be assumed lightly, for it was men as well as starfish that we sought to save. (Loren

Eiseley, *The Star Thrower* [New York: Harcourt Brace Jovanovich, 1978], 171–72, 184.)

While gatherers carry bags weighed down with the accumulation of their possessions, star throwers find their joy in picking up those who would otherwise die on the sandy beach.

Like the Star Thrower, often those who have nothing visible to show for their labors are those individuals who are filled, rewarded, and energized by a labor that invigorates, motivates, inspires, and has a purpose of such far-reaching significance that they are driven by a power beyond themselves. This power is most often felt when we are in the service of our fellow beings, for in that service, as King Benjamin taught, we are in the service of our God (see Mosiah 2:17).

We read about the pioneers who, in the early history of the Church, left their possessions, "their things," and headed west. Those who were with the handcart company who would push or pull their carts into the wilderness would give much thought to what they would make room for in their wagons and what they would be willing to leave behind. Even after the journey began, some things had to be unloaded along the way for people to reach their destination.

In our season of abundance and excess, even while we are counseled to reduce and simplify, there will be a high level of frustration until we understand the value of pruning. When someone asks the question, "How do you do it all?" our answer should be, "We don't." We must be willing to let go of many things but defend with our lives the essentials.

Now I believe it would be very easy for an inexperienced gardener to approach the task of reducing and cutting back with such vigor that he might take a saw and cut the tree down the center, through the trunk, and into the roots. Surely it would be cut back, but what of the hope for the fruit? Wise pruning, like good gardening, takes careful thought. It is only when you are clear in your mind concerning your values that you are free to simplify and reduce without putting at risk what matters most. Until we determine what is of greatest worth, we are caught up in the unrealistic idea that everything is possible.

Thomas Griffith, a contributing editor for *Time* magazine, once summarized the problem this way. Describing himself as a young man, he said:

> I thought myself happy at the time, my head full of every popular song that came along, the future before me. I could be an artist, a great novelist, an architect, a senator, a singer; having no demonstrable capacity for any of these pursuits made them all

> appear equally possible to me. All that mattered, I felt, was my inclination; I saw life as a set of free choices. Only later did it occur to me that every road taken is another untaken, every choice a narrowing. A sadder maturity convinces me that, as in a chess game, every move helps commit one to the next, and each person's situation at a given moment is the sum of the moves he has made before. (Thomas Griffith, *The Waist-High Culture* [New York: Harper and Brothers, 1949], 17.)

FOCUSING ON THE REAL ESSENTIALS

When we decide what is essential, we are released from the gripping position of doubtful indecision and confusion. It is while a person stands undecided, uncommitted, uncovenanted, with choices waiting to be made, that the vulnerability of every wind that blows becomes life threatening. Uncertainty, the thief of time and commitment, breeds vacillation and confusion.

When our choices and decisions are focused

on the accumulation of visible possessions and valuable materials, we may find that the acquisition of these things feeds an insatiable appetite and leaves us increasingly hungry. In the Book of Mormon the Lord warns us: "Wherefore, do not spend money for that which is of no worth, nor your labor for that which cannot satisfy. Hearken diligently unto me, and remember the words which I have spoken; and come unto the Holy One of Israel, and feast upon that which perisheth not, neither can be corrupted, and let your soul delight in fatness" (2 Nephi 9:51).

When our time is spent in the accumulation of experiences that nourish the spirit, we see with different glasses things that others do not see and cannot understand.

In the book *The Little Prince,* by Antoine de Saint-Exupéry, we read about the importance of values and relationships. The fox says to the Little Prince, "It is only with the heart that one can see rightly; what is essential is invisible to the eye" (Antoine de Saint-Exupéry, *The Little Prince* [New York: Harcourt, Brace, and World, 1943], 70).

One of the great examples of acquiring invisible possessions of priceless value comes from the dramatic story told of Zion's Camp. the Missouri Saints were expelled from Jackson County in late November 1833. Four months and twelve days later, on 24 February 1834, Joseph Smith was instructed to organize an army to restore the Saints to their rightful ownership of land in Jackson County. The group would march 1,000 miles in four months. They would suffer sickness, deprivation, and severe testing of every physical kind.

Heber C. Kimball said, "I took leave of my wife and children and friends, not knowing whether I would see them again in the flesh." It was not unusual for them to march thirty-five miles a day, despite blistered feet, oppressive heat, heavy rains, high humidity, hunger, and thirst. Armed guards were posted around the camp at night. At 4:00 A.M. the trumpeter roused the weary men with reveille on an old, battered French horn. Zion's Camp failed to help the Missouri Saints regain their lands and was marred by some dissension, apostasy, and unfavorable publicity, but a number of positive results came from the journey. Zion's Camp chastened, polished, and spiritually refined many of the Lord's servants. When a skeptic asked Brigham Young what he had gained from his journey, Brigham Young promptly replied, "I would not exchange the knowledge I have received this season for the whole of Geauga County" ("Church History in the Fulness of Times," prepared by the Church Educational System, Salt Lake City, Utah, 143–51).

From among the members of Zion's Camp the

Lord selected those who would lead his church during the next five decades. From the viewpoint of preparation, the Zion's Camp experiences proved to be of infinite value during the formative years of the Church. Those Saints were tried and tested. They learned what they stood for, what they were willing to live and die for, and what was of highest value.

Today our tests are different. We are not called to load our wagons and head west. Our frontier and wilderness are of a different nature, but we too must decide what we will make room for in our wagons and what is of highest value.

Recently the Museum of Church History and Art opened a new exhibit entitled "A Covenant Restored." As you enter, you begin to remember in a new way the price paid by those who came before us. Standing at the edge of a very roughhewn log cabin, you feel something of the commitment and sacrifice those early Saints made.

Erected immediately next to this very humble dwelling, where life was sustained by men and women with values, commitments, and covenants, we see a replica in actual size of the beautiful window of the historic Kirtland Temple.

As you move along the path through the museum, you are emotionally drawn from Kirtland on through the experiences that finally brought the Saints to the valley of the Great Salt Lake. At one point you see the temple as the center of everything that drove them through these incredible circumstances, and something happens inside you. I pondered the significance of the temple in their lives and ours, in ways that I hadn't before.

I stood at the side of a handcart and wondered, "How did the family decide what they would make room for in their wagons?" Then I wondered, *What will we make room for in our wagons? What is of greatest importance in life?*

One year as I was driving myself and my niece Shelly, who was then seven years old, back from a trip to Vernon, British Columbia, I had an experience that has helped me as I try to improve my ability to prune wisely and to load or unload my wagon, as the case may be.

During the trip when we were not playing the tape "Winnie the Pooh" for the hundredth time, Shelly would be asleep in the backseat of the car, and I had many hours and many miles to weigh, compare, and wonder. I had gone to Canada to take care of my sister's family of nine children while she was in the hospital with her tenth baby. After a week of doing laundry, matching socks, tending to paper routes, meals, lessons, car pooling, bedtime stories, lunch money, settling disputes over time spent in the bathroom, finding shoes, and planning for family home evening, I felt overwhelmed to say the least. At the appointed time my sister returned with a babe in arms. I stood in awe and reverence as I watched her step back into that routine with the ease and harmony of a conductor leading a well-trained orchestra with each player coming in on cue. It was a miracle to me.

As I thought of her life and mine, I began measuring what I was not doing in comparison to what she was doing. We do that, you know. I began wondering and feeling discouraged, despondent, even depressed.

At that moment, somewhere between the Canadian border and Spokane, my father's voice came into my mind. He had passed away two years before, but his voice was as clear as though he were sitting by my side. "My dear," he said, "don't worry about the little things. The big things you agreed to before you came." And for the rest of the journey, between moments of listening to "Winnie the Pooh," I asked myself over and over again, "What are the big things in life? What is essential? What is the purpose of life?" I share this experience with you, my brothers and sisters, because I believe there are times when these same questions weigh heavily on your mind.

The years have passed since that experience, and Shelly has traded Winnie the Pooh for the more important things. She has just recently received her mission call to New Zealand. She is now willing to leave important things behind, including ballroom dancing, which for Shelly borders on being essential, to go forth and teach the real essentials, the gospel of Jesus Christ. Elder John A. Widtsoe wrote:

> In our pre-existent state, in the day of the great council, we made a certain agreement with the Almighty. The Lord proposed a plan, conceived by him. We accepted it. Since the plan is intended for all men, we

> become parties to the salvation of every person under that plan. We agreed, right then and there, to be not only saviors for ourselves, but measurably saviors for the whole human family. We went into a partnership with the Lord.
>
> The working out of the plan became then not merely the Father's work, and the Savior's work, but also our work. The least of us, the humblest, is in partnership with the Almighty in achieving the purpose of the eternal plan of salvation. That places us in a very responsible attitude towards the human race.

Like the Star Thrower, it is in helping to save others that we find our pleasure and joy, our labor, and ultimately our glory. Elder Widtsoe further states:

> If the Lord's concern is chiefly to bring happiness and joy, salvation, to the whole human family, we cannot become like the Father unless we too engage in that work. There is no chance for the narrow, selfish, introspective man in the kingdom of God.

> He may survive in the world of men; he may win fame, fortune and power before men, but he will not stand high before the Lord unless he learns to do the works of God, which always points toward the salvation of the whole human family. [*Utah Genealogical and Historical Magazine,* October 1943, 190.]

Our understanding of and commitment to the covenants we have made with God are the essentials. Our day-to-day interactions, our integrity, our moral conduct, our willingness to "bear one another's burdens, that they may be light; . . . to mourn with those that mourn; . . . and comfort those that stand in need of comfort, and to stand as witnesses of God at all times and in all things, and in all places" (Mosiah 18:8–9) are at the very heart of our earth-life experience. Every decision should be made with that goal in mind, and we should expect it to be difficult, very difficult. We are to be tried and tested in all things (see D&C 136:31).

SEEING THINGS FROM AN ETERNAL PERSPECTIVE

Some time ago, my husband and I visited the Mormon cemetery at Winter Quarters, Nebraska, a monument to family members young and old buried in graves along the trail as their families continued westward toward the Rocky Mountains. Of those people who had vision and faith in God, we read:

> There are times and places in the life of every individual, every people, and every nation when great spiritual heights are reached, when courage becomes a living thing . . . when faith in God stands as the granite mountain wall, firm and immovable. . . . Winter Quarters was such a time and place for the Mormon people. [Heber J. Grant, remarks at the dedication of the Winter Quarters Monument, 1936.]

A person who only looks for the visible may draw from this pioneer experience what appears to be an obvious conclusion—families perished.

But in the eternal perspective, they did not. It was their willingness to sacrifice everything, even life if necessary, that would ensure the eternal lives of these families.

And what of our Winter Quarters and Zion's Camp experiences? Times of difficulty try the faith of all who profess to be Latter-day Saints and follow the prophets. We are walking in the well-worn paths of those who preceded us in the quest for Zion. Help and comfort are available to us through sources beyond our own immediate strength, just as they were for those who have gone before us.

It has been said that trials are at the core of saintliness. Through our covenant relationship with Jesus Christ, we do all that we can do, and by the grace of God he does the rest.

The Lord has promised us, "Come unto me, all ye that labour and are heavy laden, and I will give you rest. Take my yoke upon you, and learn of me; for I am meek and lowly in heart: and ye shall find rest unto your souls. For my yoke is easy, and my burden is light" (Matthew 11:28–30).

One of the early pioneers testified:

> I have pulled my handcart when I was so weak and weary from illness and lack of food that I could hardly put one foot ahead of the other. I have looked ahead and seen a patch of sand or a hillslope, and I have said, "I can go only that far and there I must give up for I cannot pull the load through it." . . . I have gone on to that sand and when I reached it, the cart began pushing me. I have looked back many times to see who was pushing my cart, but my eyes saw no one. I knew then that the angels of God were there. [*Relief Society Magazine,* January 1948, 8, as quoted in James E. Faust, "The Refiner's Fire," *Ensign,* May 1979, 53.]

It is with faith in God that we must condition ourselves to let go of everything if necessary. For some of us it may require unloading bad habits, attitudes, disobedience, arrogance, selfishness, and pride.

Just this summer our family came in possession of the first letter written to my grandmother by her mother when my grandmother left her home in England as a young immigrant. She left everything behind because someone taught her of the gospel of Jesus Christ. She joined the Saints in America and eventually moved to Canada. For fear of being persuaded to remain in England, she did not tell her family of her conversion to the Church or her plans to leave until after. The first letter received from her mother reads in part:

> My dearest daughter . . . whatever on earth has caused you to go out of your own country and away from all your friends, I cannot imagine. You say, "Don't fret." How do you think I can help it when such a blow as that come to struck me all up in a heap? You say you are happy, but I can't think it, for I am sure I could not have been happy to

> have gone into a foreign country and left you behind. You say you will come again, but I don't think you will hesitate your life over the deep waters again. When I think about it, I feel wretched. You had a good place and a good home to come to whenever you liked. And I must say that I loved the very ground you walked upon, and now I am left to fret in this world. But still, all the same for that, I wish you good luck and hope the Lord will prosper you in every way. I remain, your loving Mother. [Personal Files]

They never saw each other again in this earth life. And none of her family joined the Church. However, their temple work has been done for them.

What is it that drives a people to sacrifice all if necessary to receive the blessings available only in the temple? It is their faith and a spiritual witness of the importance of our covenants with God and our immense possibilities. It is in the temple, the house of the Lord, that we participate in ordinances and covenants that span the distance between heaven and earth and prepare us to return to God's presence and enjoy the blessings of eternal families and eternal life.

A few weeks after my visit to the Kirtland Temple, I was standing at the water's edge of the baptismal font in the small Manila Temple in the Philippines. Many of those dear Saints had traveled for three days in the heat and humidity by boat to come and participate in sacred ordinances available only in the temple. On one of these islands in a small, primitive nipa hut, I visited with a family of Latter-day Saints. A beautiful young fourteen-year-old in this humble setting listened intently while her father explained that in 1991, by saving all they could, the family would have enough to go to the Manila Temple, where they could be sealed as a family forever.

When we understand that our covenants with

God are essential to our eternal life, these sacred promises become the driving force that helps us lighten our load, prioritize our activities, eliminate the excesses, accelerate our progress, and reduce the distractions that could, if not guarded, get us mired down in mud while other wagons move on. If any of you are burdened with sin and sorrow, transgression and guilt, then unload your wagon and fill it with obedience, faith, and hope, and a regular renewal of your covenants with God.

President Kimball reminded us, "Since immortality and eternal life constitute the sole purpose of life, all other interests and activities are but incidental thereto" (Spencer W. Kimball, *The Miracle of Forgiveness* [Salt Lake City: Bookcraft, 1969], 2).

Does that suggest that there should be no football, fashion, fancy food, or fun? Of course not. But these things are incidental to the real purpose of our earth life. Our purpose in life provides the compass and keeps us on course while we enjoy the journey. If we are found to be long faced, sober, and sanctimonious, we will be guilty of portraying a false image of the joys of the gospel. As the pioneers traveled, there was singing and dancing. In their camaraderie, a covenant people built a community with a strong sense of brotherhood and sisterhood. People with common values and goals strengthened one another in joy and sorrow, in sickness and health. They sustained one another as they prepared to make and keep sacred covenants.

There is a unique strength that comes when a group of faithful Saints, however large or small, band together and encourage each other in righteousness.

As we take an inventory of the things we are carrying in our wagons and make decisions about what we will be willing to leave behind and what we will cling to, we have guidance. The Lord has given us a great promise to which I bear my testimony. He has said, "Therefore, if you will ask of me you shall receive; if you will knock it shall be opened unto you. Seek to bring forth and establish my Zion. Keep my commandments in all things. And, if you keep my commandments and endure to the end you shall have eternal life, which gift is the greatest of all the gifts of God" (D&C 14:5–7).

We live in a time when the things of the world would, if possible, press in upon us and close out the things of God. May we turn our attention from the glitter of the world as we give thanks for the glory of the gospel, in the name of Jesus Christ, amen.

From an address given at a Brigham Young University devotional on 13 November 1990, when Sister Kapp was serving as the general president of the Young Women of The Church of Jesus Christ of Latter-day Saints. See *Brigham Young University 1990–91 Devotional and Fireside Speeches* [1991], 41.

TAKING UPON US HIS NAME

To you student body officers who have just taken upon you the oath of office to uphold the constitution of the Associated Students of Brigham Young University and to sustain and promote the standards of The Church of Jesus Christ of Latter-day Saints, I compliment you. With that promise and commitment, may I remind you of the tremendous impact that your example can have as you bring honor and recognition to this great institution and the name *Brigham Young University.*

PREMORTAL COMMITMENTS

This year will provide for each of you a time to magnify measurably your opportunities to keep the commitments that you made before you came here to this mortal sphere.

Elder John A. Widtsoe has given us the following insight regarding those commitments that we all made. He says:

> In our pre-existent state, in the day of the great council, we made a certain agreement with the Almighty. The Lord proposed a plan conceived by him. We accepted it. Since the plan is intended for all men, we became partners to the salvation of every person under the plan. . . . We went into a partnership with the Lord. The working out of that plan became then not merely the Father's work, and the Son's work but also our work. The least of us, the humblest, is in partnership with the Almighty in achieving the purpose of the eternal plan of salvation. ["Lesson Ten, the Worth of Souls," *Utah*

Genealogical and Historical Magazine, October 1934, 189]

Relating to today's happenings, this agreement might even be considered as an oath of office. And what does it mean to be in partnership and take upon us a name?

SHELLY'S QUESTIONS

Some years ago in the early spring, I took little Shelly's hand in mine, and for hours we carefully picked our way from one rock to the next along a creek bed shaded by some tall trees. The gurgling water was like a musical accompaniment to the dance we were creating as we would take a step, hesitate, take another, and then wait a moment to secure our balance.

Before long, we were drawn to an open meadow where some large cottonwood trees had been recently cut. Making my way through the tall grass, I held Shelly's hand in mine as she cautiously placed one foot ahead of the other, walking the full length of the tree and back again. We noticed in that springtime, tender green shoots forcing their way through the earthy floor and the winter snow receding toward the mountain peaks. It seemed as though all of nature bore evidence of God's creations and his love for us.

Our afternoon activities continued until the evening breeze reminded us that our special day was coming to a close. Approaching the narrow, steep garden path leading to my home, I let go of Shelly's hand, allowing her to go first. Our hands stuck together for a moment. A bond had formed from the warmth of the day through our shared adventures.

Just before reaching the clearing near the house, we stopped. Bending down, I lifted Shelly up to see into a little nest built by a robin in the branch of a tree.

At the close of this memorable day, before

tucking my little niece (whom my sister shares with me) into bed, we knelt together while she expressed her own thanks which included the creek, the slippery rocks, the big tree, and the robin's nest. Feeling a renewed appreciation for those same wonderful blessings, I tucked the covers around her and bent down for a good-night kiss. Reaching up with both arms around my neck and pulling me close to her, Shelly whispered, "I wish we were in the same family."

"Shelly, my dear," I quickly explained, "we are in the same family."

"No, I mean the very same family. My last name is Larsen, and your last name is Kapp, and that isn't the same. I mean if you were my sister and we had the very same last name."

Even though she was very young, I felt that she might sense the security of our eternal relationship if I could awaken within her a great eternal truth.

"Shelly, we really are in the very same family. You see, we are all our Heavenly Father's children, every one of us, and that makes us in one great family. We are brothers and sisters, and Jesus is our Brother, too, our Elder Brother."

"Then, what is Jesus' last name?" she asked.

"Shelly, we know our Savior as Jesus the Christ." With the pure innocence of youth, she began to make us all one family by securing this relationship as she linked my first name with the surname "The Christ."

"On, no, my dear. We don't put our names together like that."

"But why not?" she asked.

Wanting her to be aware of the sacredness of our relationship with the Savior, I tried to explain. "I guess maybe it's because sometimes we are not good enough. I don't feel worthy yet."

With that, she raised up on her little elbow.

"What do you do that's wrong? Why don't you stop doing it, and then we can all be in the same family? We can all use his name."

As I pondered the answer to her simple questions, I heard in my mind words as though I was hearing them for the first time. And yet, it had been only two days since I had attended sacrament meeting, where I had listened to the same words. I had heard them with my ears often before, but now it seemed different. It was as though I was hearing them with my whole heart and soul:

"That they are willing to take upon them the name of thy Son, and always remember him, and keep his commandments which he has given them" (D&C 20:77).

Wasn't this the very thing that we were talking about—the responsibility of taking upon oneself that sacred name and committing to try always to remember him and keep his commandments?

It is in reaching out to others that we qualify ourselves and become more worthy of his name.

MEANING OF THE SACRAMENT

While Shelly seemed secure and satisfied with the explanation given her at that time, over the years I have searched for a deeper understanding of this sacred sacramental ordinance in which we renew our covenant each week to take upon ourselves his name. And while that usually occurs on Sunday, what does it mean on weekdays? What difference does it make to a child, a youth, or an adult? How does it affect how we live in the summer, the winter, the fall? Should it? Can we afford to consider this sacred ordinance passively and allow it to become routine in nature?

From the writings of C. S. Lewis we read, "Active habits are strengthened by repetition but passive ones are weakened. The more often [one] feels without acting, the less he will be able ever to act, and, in the long run, the less he will be able to feel" (*The Screwtape Letters* [New York: Macmillan, 1963], 70).

Jesus came into the world "to be crucified for the world, and to bear the sins of the world, and to sanctify the world, and to cleanse it from all unrighteousness; That through him all might be saved" (D&C 76:41–42).

It was Christ who suffered and died to atone for us. There is no possible way we can ransom ourselves. It was in the Garden of Gethsemane that his sufferings were beyond all mortal comprehension, that the weight of our sins caused him to feel such agony, pain, and heartbreak that he bled from every pore as he suffered, both body and spirit. When we see in our minds by the gift of the Spirit the reality of Gethsemane, it is his great love for us that gives us the strength to struggle and suffer in our small way to overcome our sins.

Can we possibly comprehend such love? It is this atonement that can, if we will just do our part, ransom us, qualify us, redeem us, save us, and exalt us. Our part, then, is to accept Christ's atonement by repenting of our sins, being baptized, receiving the Holy Ghost, and obeying all the commandments.

> We believe that through the Atonement of Christ, all mankind may be saved, by obedience to the laws and ordinances of the Gospel. [Articles of Faith 1:3]

When we became members of his Church at the time of baptism, we covenanted with the Savior to take upon ourselves his name. Do we *remember* that baptismal covenant every day—and do what we really want to do in relation to that important event in our lives?

REMINDERS

Not long ago I was sitting on the stand during the closing session of a youth conference. Just as the young priest conducting the meeting rose to his feet to bring the meeting to a close, Kathy, one of the leaders of this conference, who was sitting next to me, jumped up and unhesitatingly slipped in front of the young man. She took her place at the pulpit, faced the audience, raised both hands in front of her with outstretched fingers, and said, "I'll bet you're all wondering why I've been wearing this ugly green nail polish." A soft ripple could be heard across the audience, and I realized that I was not the only one sharing that curiosity.

"Well," she said, "it's like this: I knew my responsibilities as one of the leaders were big. I knew I had some real challenges ahead, and I didn't want to be sorry after the chance was gone that I didn't do what I really wanted to do.

"You see, I needed something that would remind me of what I really wanted to do and help me through the things I didn't want to do. So I thought of a plan. And it worked! You see," she went on, "I wanted something that would remind me of what I really wanted to make myself do. I knew my fingernails would always be there, and if they were green, I would be sure to notice them."

After giving further details and bearing a strong testimony of the joy that comes when you do what you should, she took her seat. From this insight I was reminded of the message of the Apostle Paul when he was speaking to the Corinthians and talking to them about their ways. He said, "When I was a child, I spake as a child, I understood as a child, I thought as a child: but when I became a man, I put away childish things" (1 Corinthians 13:11).

Kathy had helped us all to understand the

importance of reminders, but it was the combined voices of youth singing the closing song, resounding like a sacred sermon, that brought forth new appreciation for sacred reminders, as these wonderful young people sang:

> I marvel that he would descend from his throne divine
> To rescue a soul so rebellious and proud as mine;
> That he should extend his great love unto such as I,
> Sufficient to own, to redeem, and to justify.
>
> (*Hymns*, 190)

You and I and Shelly—all of us—have the sacrament, a holy priesthood ordinance that helps remind us of the atonement of the Savior; it helps us keep focused on our daily progress toward exaltation, to remind us of the things we really want to do and to help us through the things we don't want to do. It is a precious and sacred reminder—not just on Sunday, but on

Monday, Tuesday, and Wednesday, spring, summer, and fall, when we're on the mountain peaks of our lives, and also when we're in the valleys. What is true for Shelly and you and me is that our Savior loves us very much.

ACTIVE PARTICIPATION

Speaking of the Son of God, Alma, in the Book of Mormon, had this to say: "And he shall go forth, suffering pains and afflictions and temptations of every kind; . . . he will take upon him the pains and the sicknesses of his people. . . . and he will take upon him their infirmities, that his bowels may be filled with mercy, according to the flesh, that he may know according to the flesh how to succor his people according to their infirmities" (Alma 7:11–12).

President Marion G. Romney's insight has made a change in my life regarding the opportunity that is mine to partake of the sacrament. May I share it with you:

> Now, partaking of the sacrament is not to be a mere passive experience. We are not to remember the Lord's suffering and death only as we may remember some purely secular historical event. Participating in the sacrament service is meant to be a vital and spiritualizing experience. Speaking of it, the Savior said:
>
> And it shall be a testimony unto the Father that ye do always remember me. [3 Nephi 18:7]

Then President Romney continued:

> In order to testify, one's mind has to function, and it must be concentrated upon the thing to be testified. And we are not only to partake of the emblems of the sacrament in remembrance of the Redeemer, testifying that we do always remember him, but we are also thereby to witness unto the Father that we are willing to take upon us the name of his Son and that we will keep his commandments. . . .
>
> Now there is a doctrine abroad in the world today which teaches that the physical

> emblems of the sacrament are transformed into the flesh and blood of Jesus. We do not teach such doctrine, for we know that any transformation which comes from the administration of the sacrament takes place in the souls of those who understandingly partake of it. It is the participating individuals who are affected, and they are affected in a most marvelous way, for they are given the Spirit of the Lord to be with them. [In Conference Report, April 1946, 39–40]

At those very times, brothers and sisters, when you and I feel least comfortable about carrying his holy name and have the keenest sense of our imperfections—those moments when the flesh is weak, and our spirit suffers disappointment, knowing what we can become, we might feel a sense of withdrawing, a pulling away, a feeling of needing to set aside for a time at least that divine relationship with the Savior, until we are more worthy—at such moments, the offer is there to accept the great gift of the Atonement even before we change. When you feel the need to pull away, will you reach out to him? Instead of feeling the need to resist, will you submit to his will?

It is in our struggles, while striving to qualify, that our spirits reach out in greater humility and gratitude, and we are better prepared to receive the gift because we so desperately need it—in fact, we must have it if we are to receive our eternal rewards.

A PRECIOUS GIFT

When my father was in the last stages of stomach cancer, his body wasting away—then weighing less than one hundred pounds—his spirit growing in strength every single day, he shared with me his new insights from that perspective.

"It is a fact," he bore witness, "that the body and the spirit are separate. When this process of separation is witnessed firsthand," he said with conviction and even enthusiasm, "the meaning of eternal life and the resurrection takes on a new dimension of understanding. It is like discovering a precious gift you've held in your possession all this time but never unwrapped; and then the time comes when you open it, and you're more ready to fully appreciate the divine nature of the gift because you are prepared to use it for the purpose for which it was intended."

The purpose of the sacramental covenant is always in force. That gift becomes more precious when we don't leave it wrapped, but rather prepare ourselves to use it for the purpose for which it was intended. I would say now to Shelly, "Yes, my dear, put my name with the Savior's." He said we could. He wants us to feel comfortable carrying his name.

We must come to the sacramental altar hungry—a spiritual hunger and thirst for righteousness. It is a time for self-evaluation, a time to rectify our courses, if necessary, and to make right our lives. It is a time and place for us to judge ourselves and come to better understand the magnitude of that sacred divine gift and the reality of being allowed to have his Spirit with us always to direct every act of our lives.

I believe that each new day can be faced with greater anticipation and purpose when we are reminded of the words of Elder John A. Widtsoe:

> There is a spiritual meaning of all human acts and earthly events. . . . No man is quite so happy, I think, as he who backs all his labors by . . . a spiritual interpretation and understanding of the acts of life. A piece of silver always has a certain value as it passes from hand to hand; it is weighed and we sell it in the marketplace, but, when that piece of silver is coined into a dollar, it receives the stamp of government service; it becomes a

> coin of the realm, and it moves from hand to hand to accomplish the work of the realm. So, every act of man, the moment it is fitted into the great plan, the plan of salvation, receives spiritual coinage, and passes from hand to hand, from mind to mind, to accomplish the great work of God. [In Conference Report, April 1922, 96–97.]

PARTNERSHIP WITH THE SAVIOR

As we gradually move to that spiritual level, we will begin to experience that partnership to which we agreed in our premortal experience—to help to bring salvation and eternal life to everyone under the plan.

When Christ becomes our constant companion, it will make our whole day different, and with his Spirit reflected in our language, in our daily work, at school, on the highway, in the marketplace, slowly, day by day, our conduct will become more unselfish, our relationships more tender, our desire to serve more constant, and we will find ourselves going about doing good. Always. We will have taken upon us not only his name, but his image in our countenances also (see Alma 5:14).

This experiment has been tried before, even in Christ's lifetime. A few men were admitted to the inner circle of friendship and, day by day, his first disciples became more mellow and softened and began to grow spiritually with power and strength and influence.

For the Apostle Paul, the process was more dramatic. On the road to Damascus he met the Savior, and from that time his words, his deeds, his career, his daily walk were different.

Have we experienced this encounter on our Damascus road? Or maybe in a less dramatic way? When it happens we will be allowed to witness miracles. We will better understand them; in fact, we will participate in them. Lives will be changed when we begin to see each other more as our Savior sees us. We will want to teach each other the way he would teach us. We will yearn for the spirituality to bear testimony of the things to which he bears testimony. And when we meet, it will be as someone said: "We will not just exchange words; what we will exchange is souls." Not just with our friends and loved ones, but with every person for whose eternal welfare we share a responsibility. With his Spirit we will be allowed to see things—not as the world sees them, but more as he would see them. We will learn to hearken to the voice of the Spirit.

INFLUENCE OF THE SPIRIT

President Marion G. Romney, in speaking to a group of sisters who were being released from their callings in the Church a few years ago, said to us in part, "I pray that the Lord will help you to live every day so that you can have the Spirit of the Lord with you. It is a wonderful thing to try to know and to try to live so that you can *hear* and respond to the voice of the Lord. That's where the comfort comes in this life. Hearken to the voice of the Spirit, and have the discernment to know what the Spirit tells you. Then have the courage to follow that counsel."

One day I witnessed evidence of the Spirit and the courage to follow the counsel. It was in a second-grade elementary classroom. The student teacher held the children captive with her story-telling skills. In great detail, she told of a cross old man whose name was Mr. Black. In contrast, the account was given in similar detail of a Mr. Brown, who was kind and thoughtful and loved by everyone. At the conclusion of the story, the teacher asked the children, "How many of you would like to have Mr. Brown for a neighbor?" Every hand in the room was raised. Then, almost as an afterthought, she asked the question, "And is there anyone who would like to have Mr. Black for a neighbor?"

A little boy in a faded green shirt near the back of the room began to raise his hand, bringing a ripple of quiet amusement from the children. Hesitating only briefly, he looked around at his friends and still mustered the courage to hold his hand high and dare to stand alone in his difference. When called on for an explanation of his single vote, he spoke in a soft tone. "Well," he said, "I'd like Mr. Black to be my neighbor because if he was my neighbor, my mom would make a cake for me to take to him, and then he wouldn't be that way anymore." A hush fell over the room. Everyone felt something wonderful that they couldn't explain. A little child broke the silence like a benediction: "Oh . . . I wish I'd said that."

We had all made a quick decision about who would be the best neighbor, but only one—just one—had a spirit within, the discernment that allowed him to see what might be.

Another day I witnessed the need for the Spirit to help guide the service that was being performed by well-meaning neighbors. A widow lady said to me, "I don't need more food. My freezer is literally full of the neighbors' cakes and pies and goodies. But I need for someone to invite me to go to Temple Square with them and their children to see the Christmas lights. You don't really see the lights without the children."

Sometimes it's cake, but sometimes it isn't. It is the Spirit that will help us customize our service.

CHANGE OF HEART

As President Spencer W. Kimball once said, "God does notice us, and he watches over us. But it is usually through another person that he meets our needs" ("Small Acts of Service,"

Ensign, December 1974, 5). I believe it is one who hears and hearkens when the Lord speaks.

Consider now, even at this moment, the brother and sister sitting next to you, or the one nearby, through the hall, across the street, or down the road. Will you put yourself so in tune that you can try to see in that person what the Savior sees? Will you share with that brother or sister something that would ease a heavy load, brighten a dark day, expand a limited vision, or vitalize a dying hope, and try to do it the way you think the Savior might do it? Could you? Would you?

Given the opportunities available to each one of us this very week to live the sacramental life, can you feel within a growing strength, a yearning desire, an increased commitment to reach out? Will you consider seriously what truth of which you have a personal witness that you could teach another? And teach it in *partnership* with the Savior, even to the person sitting next to you who might be a stranger even though a brother or sister?

I tell you, if you will sincerely try to do this, something sweet and gentle will surround you. Voices will be softened, hearts touched, and a deep feeling of caring will swell up within. You will feel the Spirit even as you serve in his name. It will be a spiritual experience, the kind we yearn for and can have when we remember him and have his Spirit with us.

It is in reaching out to others that we qualify ourselves and become more worthy of his name. Our ordinary work, our routine duties, and our familiar relationships can become more sacramental in nature.

One day I experienced that great joy while casually sitting by a friend who had recently been called as mission president, and I thought, "What could I share with him that would help at this important time in his life?" I endeavored to see in this friend what I thought the Lord might see in him. I desired to say what would be of importance to him at this time. I had a wonderful feeling of love for my longtime friend come into my heart, and I was prompted to share with him the thoughts that had come into my mind.

"I guess at a time like this," I said, "one feels an increased urgency to have a pure vessel through which the Spirit can work unrestrained. Yet, isn't it a marvelous thing to know that you will have access to that great power, that inspiration, and even revelation every day while yet you and your missionaries are striving for perfection?"

Almost immediately his eyes were moist. His chin began to quiver, and he said, "You must have known I needed to hear that."

When we are in the church, on the bus, in the grocery store, in the classroom, and, most importantly, in our homes, let us strive to see each other the way we think he might, and, sensing that person's divine potential, let us take the opportunity to teach an eternal truth that will be personalized because the Spirit prompts us.

In the closing moments of the Savior's life, while he suffered for us, he told us how we can be disciples for him: "A new commandment I give unto you, That ye love one another; as I have loved you, that ye also love one another. By this shall all men know that ye are my disciples, if ye have love one to another" (John 13:34–35).

Every act of our lives *can* become a sacramental experience when we take upon us his name; and when our performance falls short in spite of our striving for perfection, we will find ourselves eagerly and anxiously and more gratefully than ever before, drawn to the Sabbath day and the sacramental altar where we can feel the glorious transformation of the healing of our wounded spirits as we commit to strive again and again to follow him.

With a new day and a new week and a new opportunity, we will welcome another chance to feel more deeply, to care more sincerely, to understand more compassionately, to teach more purposefully, to remember him always, and to have his Spirit to be with us.

As I held Shelly's little hand in mine for one last squeeze before tiptoeing from her room that evening some years ago, a feeling of gratitude and reverence came flooding forth as I realized that—while her hand had been in mine for most of the afternoon as I helped her through the creek, across the rocks, and along the fallen tree trunk, and lifted her up to see the miracle of life unfolding in a robin's nest—this child had led me to begin a search that would lift me up to a better understanding of a great eternal truth. King Benjamin explained it for us: "And now, because of the covenant which ye have made ye shall be called the children of Christ, his sons, and his daughters; for behold, this day he hath spiritually begotten you; for ye say that your hearts are changed through faith on his name; therefore, ye are born of him and have become his sons and his daughters" (Mosiah 5:7).

Brothers and sisters, we can all be members of the same family. If you're doing something you shouldn't, consider Shelly's question to me, "Why don't you stop?" It may not always be easy, but with his help we can overcome.

I bear my witness to the reality of our eternal brotherhood and sisterhood, and extend my love unto each of you, my brothers and sisters, in the name of Jesus Christ, whose name we are privileged to bear, amen.

This devotional address was delivered at Brigham Young University on 5 May 1981, when Sister Kapp was serving as a member of the Curriculum Planning Committee of The Church of Jesus Christ Latter-day Saints. See *Speeches of the Year, 1981* [1982], 77.